Being Billy

Story by Dianne Wolfer

Illustrations by Meredith Thomas

Being Billy

Text: Dianne Wolfer
Illustrations: Meredith Thomas
Editor: Joanna Rohan
Design: Goanna Graphics (Vic) Pty Ltd
Reprint: Siew Han Ong

PM Plus
Sapphire Level 30

ISBN 978 0 17 010811 9
ISBN 978 0 17 010812 6 (set)

Cengage Learning Australia
Level 7, 80 Dorcas Street
South Melbourne, Victoria Australia 3205
Phone: 1300 790 853

Cengage Learning New Zealand
Unit 4B Rosedale Office Park
331 Rosedale Road, Albany, North Shore NZ 0632
Phone: 0508 635 766

For learning solutions, visit **cengage.com.au**

Printed in China by 1010 Printing International Ltd
31 22

Contents

Chapter 1

Billy and Andrew

Billy loved his big brother Andrew. No one else in the world was as clever and wonderful. When they were together, Billy forgot that he was different.

Billy and Andrew did exciting things together. Things like building forts and catching yabbies. But what he liked most was putting on plays with Andrew and his friend, Gino. Throughout the summer holidays, the three of them made costumes and props, and performed shows for their parents or Gino's dog, Bluey.

Usually, Billy looked forward to the end of the holidays. He liked shopping for the new school year. This year there was more to buy because Andrew was going to a new school.

"I wish I could go to high school with you," Billy said. "I'll have no one to sit with on the bus."

"What about Gino? He'll be catching your bus to college."

"It won't be the same."

"Never mind. Only another year, then you'll be at high school, too. Besides, you can help with the school play this year. Mrs Robinson always needs people to help backstage."

"Maybe I could have the lead role."

Andrew smiled. "Maybe."

That was in January. Since then, Andrew had made new friends at high school and everything had changed. He went to the movies or the mall all the time, and never invited Billy.

Sometimes Mum made him take Billy, but Andrew's high school friends always stared at him and ignored him. That made Billy mad. Just because he wasn't the same as them didn't mean they could treat him that way.

Billy felt lonely. The kids at his school were usually friendly, but he'd never had a best friend. That was one of the problems when you were different.

Chapter 2

Billy on His Own

The Easter holidays came and went. Sometimes Gino and Billy got together, but it wasn't as much fun without Andrew.

Things became steadily worse. When Andrew and Billy went to the supermarket, Andrew refused to give Billy rides on the trolley. "We're too old for that Billy," he said. When Billy tried to hold hands, Andrew pulled away. "Only little kids do that," he said. "Besides your palms are all sweaty!" Billy wiped his hands on his jeans. Andrew had never complained about his palms before.

Billy watched Andrew. He studied his brother, looking for a sign that he was back to his old self. But all Andrew wanted was to be left alone. Billy tried leaving hints. He left their best costumes on Andrew's bed, but Andrew pushed them away. He left their photo album open at his favourite page – the picture of Bluey standing on their best fort – but Andrew ignored it.

Billy kept trying to get Andrew's attention. One day, Andrew did notice.

“Stop sneaking around after me,” Andrew shouted. “I’m sick of you staring at me all the time. Why can’t you just leave me alone?’

Billy knew Andrew had had enough of him. There’s no point crying over spilt milk, their mother always said. So Billy decided he’d have to find something fun he could do on his own. When Mrs Robinson announced the upcoming school play, the timing seemed perfect.

“We’ll be performing ‘Midnite’. It’s an olden-day story about a bushranger and his animal gang. Here is a list of the characters. We’ll read the play after lunch. Rehearsals will be held after school if you want to try out for a part. We’ll also need people to help with costumes, painting sets, lighting and stage management. I want everyone to be involved!’

Billy looked at the list of characters and Sally helped him read them. Sally sat beside him in class.

"I'm going to try out for the part of Khat," she said. "Do you want to act or have a job backstage?" Billy smiled. Most people would expect him to take an easy job, but Sally never assumed he couldn't do things. Billy remembered acting in plays through summer with Gino and Andrew.

"I want to act," he whispered. "Good for you," Sally replied. "Who do you want to be?" "Someone important!" Billy said.

"What about the lead role, Captain Midnite?" "Perfect," Billy answered, turning his head dramatically. They giggled until Mrs Robinson told them off.

Chapter 3

Rehearsing

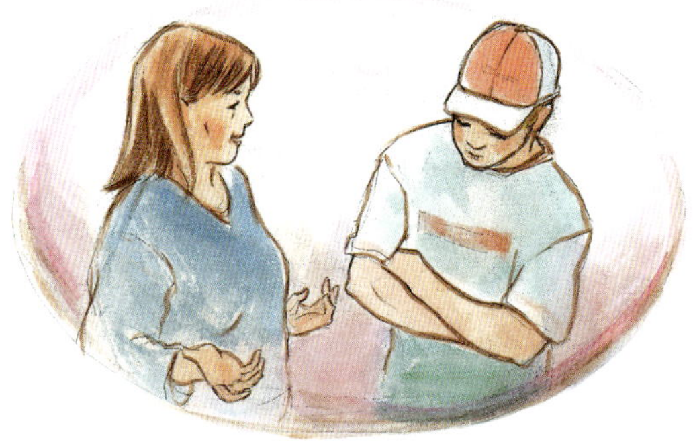

"Have you heard Billy's news?" their mother asked Andrew.

Andrew sighed.

Their mother gave him a sharp look. "Your brother has landed the main role in the school play."

"You're joking? As if they'd give it to him!" Andrew replied nastily.

"Andrew, you may be too self-involved to notice, but your brother is actually a very talented actor."

Andrew snorted. "He'll just make a fool of himself. And us!"

The back door banged and Andrew looked up. His brother was staring at him – a look of disbelief and betrayal on his face.

"It's not often that I'm ashamed of you, Andrew," their mother said quietly, "but I am today. The main reason Billy auditioned was to impress you."

Andrew scowled and slunk off to his room. Stupid play, he thought. He sat on the bed sorting his football cards. "Someone has to have the guts to tell the truth," he muttered.

Billy stopped following Andrew around. At first Andrew was relieved, but after a while he felt guilty. He offered to help Billy learn his lines. If Billy was determined to act in public, at least he could try to minimise the damage.

"That's okay," Billy said. "Mrs Robinson and Mum are helping. Besides, I already know most of the words."

Andrew put away his football cards. He picked up their photo album and opened it at the picture of Bluey on their fort. "He'll soon forget what I said," Andrew told himself. "Billy never holds grudges."

Billy became busy with rehearsals. He loved pretending to be a bushranger, especially when his gang got to hold up stagecoaches.

"Stand and deliver!" they shouted and Billy knew his voice was the loudest.

Mrs Robinson spent time working with him. She taught Billy when to overact dramatically for laughs, and when to understate his lines for quiet impact. Her patience encouraged Billy to experiment. Soon he was able to help the other kids when they forgot their lines.

Unfortunately Sally wasn't chosen for the role of Khat. Mrs Robinson said she could be Dora, the cow. But Sally didn't want to be a cow, so she became a trooper.

During Act One, she had to chase Billy across the stage. Sometimes, during lunchtimes, Sally and her friends practised that scene, and then let Billy hang around until the bell rang. Even though he missed the bus ride with Andrew, this was the happiest Billy had ever been at school.

Chapter 4

Stealing the Show

The days before the concert whizzed by and Billy started to get nervous. Andrew's words kept playing on his mind.

"Do *you* think I'll make a fool of myself?" he asked Mum one evening.

Mum hugged him. "Of course not. Mrs Robinson is proud of you. She said this play will be the best she's ever produced!"

"But Andrew still thinks I'll embarrass us, doesn't he?"

Mum hesitated. "Anything we do embarrasses Andrew at the moment," she sighed. "Don't worry. He'll settle down."

Mum turned off the light and Billy lay awake in the dark. He wanted Andrew to enjoy the play and not be embarrassed that Captain Midnite was his brother.

* * *

As soon as he pulled on his costume, Billy's nerves disappeared. His Akubra hat, checked shirt and farm boots made him feel special, but it was the eye mask that Billy really loved. When he wore it, he looked like the other kids.

Billy grinned at Khat, Red Ned and the rest of his gang. They walked onto the stage and Billy 'became' his character. As he rode through the Hidden Valley, Billy felt the wind in his hair. When Captain Midnite shook hands with Trooper O'Grady, Billy felt their friendship. And when Captain Midnite fell in love with Miss Laura Wellborn, Billy felt his cheeks blush.

Then it was over. The audience cheered and Billy scanned the crowd for Andrew. Andrew was clapping, but the blinding spotlight made it hard for Billy to see his brother's face. They ran offstage. Then the audience stood, cheering even more loudly.

"Go back and bow again," Mrs Robinson whispered.

They ran back and bowed. Then Mrs Robinson skipped out and she bowed too.

Mrs Robinson pretended not to notice the boy offstage balancing a huge bouquet of flowers, until he stumbled out to present them to her. The audience cheered again.

"Andrew, can you go backstage and find Billy?" Mum asked. "I have to talk to Mr Malouf about Billy's sports program."

Billy this, Billy that, Andrew thought. How come it's always Billy that gets the attention? He kicked a loose floorboard, amazed that his brother had done so well.

Things were mayhem backstage and Billy was in the midst of it.

"Well done!" Mrs Robinson gushed as she kissed Billy on the cheek. A tall man beside her coughed. "Oh, that's right," she said. "Billy, I want to introduce you to Mr Fox. He works for Channel 5 TV. He'd like to talk to you."

Andrew pricked up his ears. Mr Fox held out his hand and Billy shook it up and down energetically. Andrew looked away in embarrassment. Why did Billy always have to get so excited?

"Great performance, Billy," Mr Fox said. Billy beamed proudly. "Do you know the show *Here and There*?" Mr Fox continued.

"Do I know it?" Billy shouted. "I watch it every night! Actually I'm in love with Kylie Minnow!" he whispered.

Andrew rolled his eyes.

"You and every other boy," Mr Fox laughed. "Well, Billy, I was very impressed with your performance tonight. My niece Sally was …"

"I know Sally," Billy interrupted. "She's a trooper."

"Yes, she is. Anyway, Billy, I'm glad I came to watch Sally. You see, we've been looking for someone like you to play a new character on *Here and There*. We need a twelve-year-old boy to play Kylie's brother."

Billy shook his head. "But Kylie doesn't have a brother."

"Ah, that's what everyone thinks! He's been living in the country with Kylie's grandma. Soon he'll be moving to Winter Creek to go to high school."

"I'm twelve next month," Billy remarked.

"Yes," Mr Fox said with a smile. "Mrs Robinson told me."

Mr Fox then spoke to Mum and arranged an interview and screen test. Then Mr Fox rang and asked them to come back for another meeting.

"Billy's a natural," he said. "The screen test was excellent. Billy is exactly what we've been looking for. We want to offer him a contract."

Chapter 5

Here and There

Soon after the play, Billy was being picked up by a Channel 5 driver and taken to the set of *Here and There*. School even let him take time off for filming!

When Billy received free passes for friends to watch the filming, he immediately asked Andrew and Gino to come along.

Andrew and Gino were allowed half a day off school. They left at lunchtime and caught the bus to the set. A security guard was blocking the gate. He looked the boys up and down, then raised his eyebrows. Gino pushed Andrew forward.

"No entry for autographs," the guy barked. "You'll have to wait until they finish. He looked at his watch and then at their uniforms. "So, if I were you, I'd get back to school before the teachers notice that you're gone." The security guard adjusted his black t-shirt and turned to leave.

"You don't understand," Andrew said. "We know one of the actors. He invited us to come and watch them filming."

"Yeah sure, kid. If I had a buck for every time I heard that, I'd be rich."

"Show him the passes," Gino whispered.

Andrew fumbled in his pocket. "Wait," he called. "Look – we have passes."

The guard turned around. He examined the passes, then smiled. “Why didn’t you say so in the first place?” He pushed a button and the heavy gate slid open. “So, who do you know? Hang on, don’t tell me … You look a bit like Kylie Minnow. I bet you’re her kid brother.”

Andrew blushed. “Not quite. I’m Billy Rose’s brother.”

The guard frowned. “Billy Rose?” Then he grinned. “Billy! You mean the new kid? The one with the great smile?”

Andrew hesitated. He'd expected him to say, Billy, the one with Down's Syndrome. That's how people usually described his brother. Andrew pictured Billy's face. He remembered the way Billy smiled when they went fishing. The guard was right – Billy did have a great smile. It lit up his whole face. "Yep, that's the one," he mumbled, realising that he hadn't shared many of Billy's smiles lately.

"Which way do we go?" Gino asked the guard.

"See that caravan over there by the trees?" Gino nodded. "Well, they should be filming on the other side of it. Down by the creek."

"Let's go." Gino grabbed Andrew's arm and dragged him towards the caravan.

Billy was sitting amidst a group of actors. As they walked closer, Andrew heard them talking and laughing together.

"Hey, look!" Gino gasped. "That's Kylie Minnow. Wow! She looks even better in real life."

Andrew didn't answer. He was watching Billy whisper something to Kylie. Andrew stared. His brother, Billy, was chatting to Kylie Minnow and she was hanging off every word!

Andrew thought about how he'd been treating Billy lately. He remembered how he'd said Billy would embarrass them at the school play. Then he remembered how he'd ignored Billy at the mall. He remembered pretending not to notice his new friends making fun of him.

Then he remembered the look of hurt that crossed Billy's face when he'd realised that his big brother wasn't so special after all.

"Hey, what's wrong?" Gino asked. "C'mon, let's go and get their autographs."

Andrew shrugged. He couldn't go over. He was too embarrassed to tell Gino that, while he'd been showing off with his new friends, his brother had quietly got on with his own life. Andrew hung his head. His brother was indeed the real star here.

Billy turned around and saw Andrew and Gino. A huge grin appeared on his face. "Andrew!" he yelled. Kylie looked up as Billy knocked over a chair hurrying to greet his older brother.

"I told Kylie you'd be here soon," Billy said, tugging Andrew's arm. "Come and meet everyone."

"In a moment, Billy. First … I want to say, umm … I want to say that …"

"Ten minutes until your scene, Billy," a girl called.

Billy studied Andrew's eyes, then smiled. "It's okay," he said. "I think I understand."

Billy grabbed Andrew's hand, then remembering his brother's words at the supermarket, he let go. Andrew blushed. "I'm sorry, Billy, but we really are a bit too old to hold hands," he said. "But hey, I think it's okay for us to do this." He let his arm rest loosely over Billy's shoulders.

Billy beamed. "Okay!" he said. "Now, come on. I want you to meet my new friends!"